# Wonders

McGraw Hill Education

**Cover and Title Page:** Nathan Love

# www.mheonline.com/readingwonders

Mc Graw Hill Education

ISBN: 978-0-02-130544-5
MHID: 0-02-130544-7

Printed in the United States of America.

10 LKV 25                                    C

# Wonders

# ELD
## Companion Worktext

**Program Authors**

Diane August

Jana Echevarria

Josefina V. Tinajero

Mc Graw Hill Education

# Unit 4

# IT'S UP TO YOU

# IT'S UP TO YOU

## THE BIG IDEA

**How do we decide what's important?**

ZUMA Press/Newscom

### Essential Question

**What kinds of stories do we tell? Why do we tell them?**

**≫** *Go Digital*

4

**What does the boy do to tell a story? Write words in the chart to describe different ways people tell stories.**

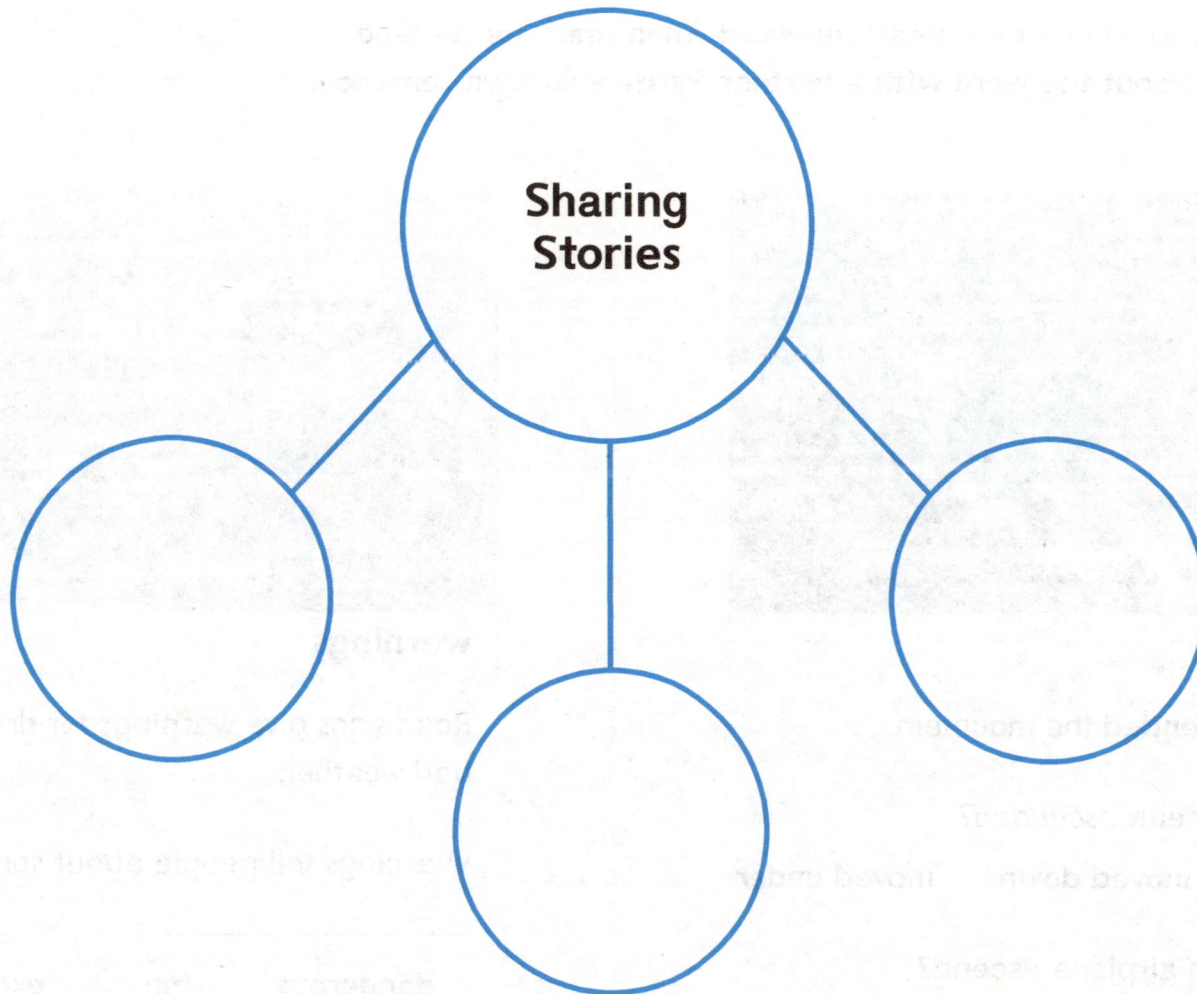

**Sharing Stories**

**Discuss the different ways people tell stories. Use words from the chart. Complete the sentence:**

The boy is _____ to tell a story.

People tell stories by _____.

# More Vocabulary

Look at the picture. Read the word. Then read the sentence.
Talk about the word with a partner. Write your own sentence.

**ascended**

The hikers ascended the mountain.

What words mean *ascended*?

**moved up**    **moved down**    **moved under**

**When does an airplane ascend?**

An airplane ascends when _____

_____.

**warnings**

Road signs give warnings for drivers during bad weather.

Warnings tell people about something

_____.

**dangerous    fun    exciting**

**What do signs at the beach give warnings about?**

The signs at the beach give warnings for

people to _____.

# Words and Phrases: *along* and *aside*

The word *along* means "in the direction of."

Where are the people walking?

The people are walking **along** the path.

The word *aside* means "moved to the side or away from you."

Where did the cars move?

The large truck moved **aside** to let the cars pass.

**COLLABORATE** Talk with a partner. Look at the picture. Read the sentence. Write the word that completes the sentence.

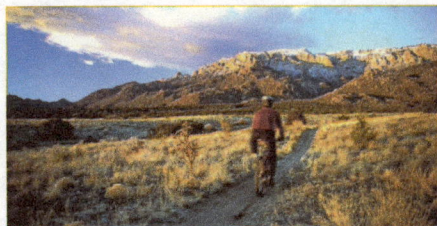

The man is riding _____ the bike path.

**along**          **aside**

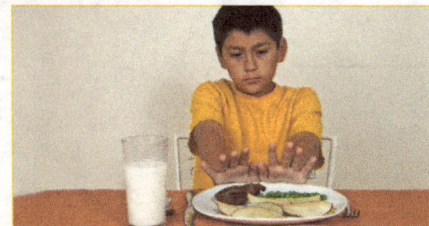

The boy pushed the plate _____ because he was not hungry.

**along**          **aside**

**COLLABORATE**

**1 Talk About It**

Look at the picture. Read the title. Talk about what you see. Use these words.

**train    girl    lifting    strong**

Write about what you see.

The story is about _____

_____

_____.

What is the girl doing?

The girl is _____

_____.

Why is she unusual?

She is unusual because _____

_____.

Take notes as you read the story.

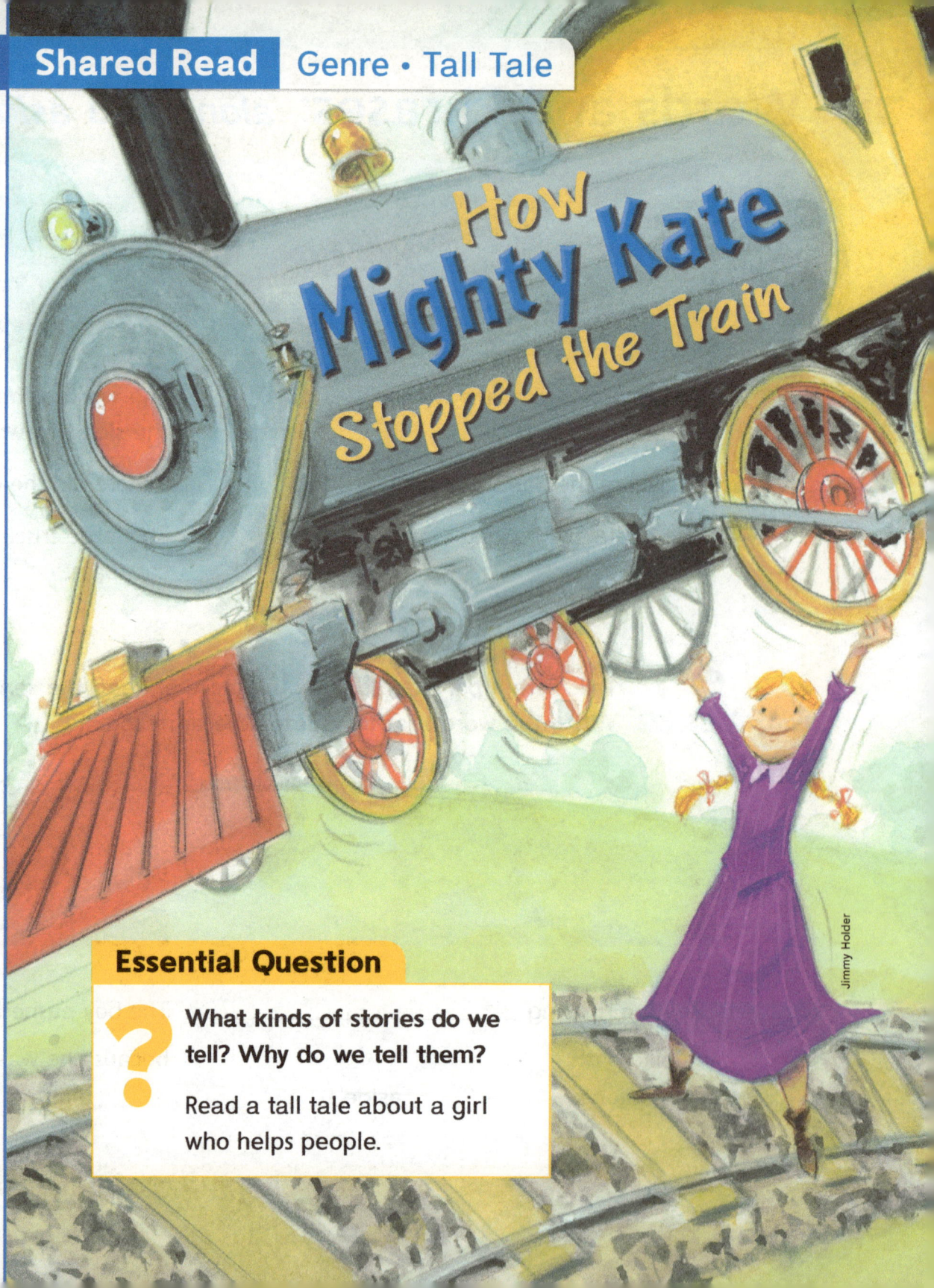

# How Mighty Kate Stopped the Train

Jimmy Holder

**Essential Question**

**?** **What kinds of stories do we tell? Why do we tell them?**

Read a tall tale about a girl who helps people.

Railroad trains probably pass through your neck of the woods. But this story takes place when railroads were new in the American South.

This is the amazing tale of a strong young gal who folks called "Mighty Kate." She got the nickname when she was born because she was so strong. When the doctor weighed her on a scale, the tiny baby lifted the doctor to weigh him!

Mighty Kate impressed people as she grew up. If Kate saw a boulder in her path, she just lifted that huge rock, tossed it aside, and sauntered off. Once, her father's horse and buggy got stuck in a ditch. Mighty Kate pulled them both out of the ditch. She used just one hand!

When Mighty Kate was 15 years old, there was a powerful storm. Homes shook in fear, and trees ran for their lives! Mighty Kate saw a train crossing Creek Bridge. Suddenly there was a thunderous crash. The noise caused the weeping willows to weep so hard that their tears flooded the entire area!

# Text Evidence

## 1 Specific Vocabulary A C T

The expression *neck of the woods* means "an area." What does the sentence tell about the neck of the woods? Underline the text.

## 2 Sentence Structure A C T

Reread the second sentence in the third paragraph. What did Kate do if she saw a boulder? Circle the three verbs that tell you. What does the word *If* tell you about the event?

The word *if* tells that the event

_____

## 3 Comprehension
## Point of View

Reread the fourth paragraph. Put a box around sentences that describe things like people. Why does the narrator do this? Support your answer with text evidence.

The narrator wants to _____

_____

9

# Text Evidence

## 1 Sentence Structure A C T

Reread the last sentence in the first paragraph. How did Kate use her arms? Underline the text.

Kate used one arm to _____

_____ and the other

arm to _____.

## 2 Comprehension
## Point of View

Reread the second paragraph. Why was Kate "not finished?" Circle the text that tells you.

Kate was not finished because

_____

_____

**COLLABORATE**

## 3 Talk About It

Discuss why the narrator says "There was no time to waste!"

There was no time to waste

because _____.

Mighty Kate ran outside and saw the bridge and train in the creek. Kate grabbed a vine and slid down to the creek. Two railroad workers were trapped under a pile of rails. Kate swept away all the rails with one arm. Whoosh! The men were free. She pulled up each worker and **ascended** the vine with the other hand—no exaggeration!

Mighty Kate was not finished. She knew the 10:30 train was coming, and it was filled with passengers. Kate had to tell workers at the nearest train station to stop the train because the bridge was out. However, the nearest station was an hour away. There was no time to waste!

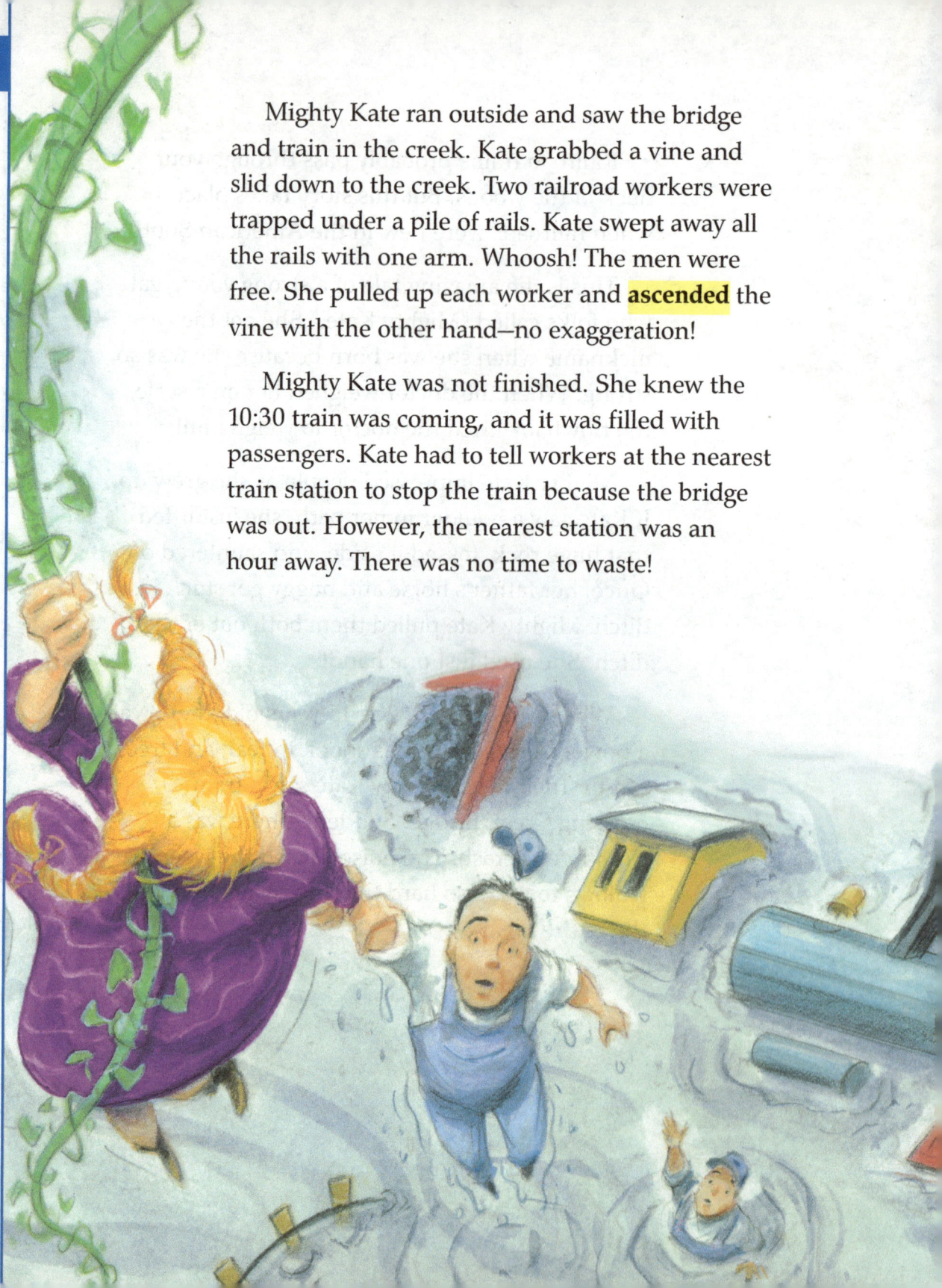

Mighty Kate ran toward the train station while wind and rain attacked her. She started to cross River Bridge when floodwaters rushed into the river. Suddenly, Kate saw a huge log floating in the river. It was moving toward the bridge and her!

Mighty Kate grabbed the log. She began to wring the wood with her bare hands. Soon the log turned into a shriveled twig!

Mighty Kate crossed the bridge and ran into the train station, but the train had already left. Kate ran after it, but she couldn't catch up to it. Then she got an idea. She whistled so loudly that the train engineer heard it and stopped the train.

Kate told the engineer that Creek Bridge was out. The engineer thanked the brave young girl who had saved the day.

Today we have whistles on trains to give warnings along the track! And this is all because of Mighty Kate.

## Make Connections

**?** Discuss how the author told the story. Why do you think the author told the story this way? ESSENTIAL QUESTION

What stories do you like to tell to people? How do you tell them? TEXT TO SELF

# Text Evidence 🔍

**1 Sentence Structure** A C T

Reread the first sentence. Circle the text that tells what Kate was doing. Underline the text that tells what was happening to Kate. What word tells the two events happened at the same time?

I know because _____

_____.

**2 Specific Vocabulary** A C T

The phrase *saved the day* means "solved a big problem." How did Kate save the day? Circle the text that tells you.

Kate saved the day by _____

_____.

**3 Comprehension**
**Point of View**

Reread the last paragraph. Put a box around the text that tells the narrator's point of view.

Jimmy Holder

# Respond to the Text

COLLABORATE **Partner Discussion** Work with a partner. Read the questions about "How Mighty Kate Stopped the Train." Show where you found text evidence. Write the page numbers. Then discuss what you read.

---

**What was special about Kate as a child?**

I read that Kate got her name because _____.

When Kate was a baby, she lifted _____.

Kate saved a horse and buggy by _____.

**Text Evidence**

Page(s): _____

Page(s): _____

Page(s): _____

---

**How did Kate stop the train?**

Kate saved two men by _____.

Then Kate ran to _____.

Kate whistled so that _____.

The story is a tall tale because the details are _____
_____.

**Text Evidence**

Page(s): _____

Page(s): _____

Page(s): _____

Page(s): _____

---

COLLABORATE **Group Discussion** Present your answers to the group. Cite text evidence for your ideas. Listen to and discuss the group's opinions.

**Write** Work with a partner. Look at your notes about "How Mighty Kate Stopped the Train." Write your answer to the Essential Question. Use text evidence to support your answer. Use vocabulary words in your writing.

How is "How Mighty Kate Stopped the Train" a tall tale?

"How Mighty Kate Stopped the Train" is a tall tale because _____

_____.

I know this because details about Kate _____

_____.

The narrator exaggerates details by _____

_____.

**Share Writing** Present your writing to the class. Discuss their opinions. Talk about their ideas. You can say:

I agree with _____.

I do not agree because _____.

# Write to Sources

Karim

**Take Notes About the Text** I took notes about the text on the idea web to answer the question: *Is Mighty Kate stronger than other people?*

pages 8–11

**Clue**
Baby Kate lifted a doctor. Other babies cannot lift people.

**Conclusion**
Mighty Kate is stronger than other people.

**Clue**
Kate lifted and threw a boulder. Most people cannot lift or throw a boulder.

**Clue**
Kate pulled a horse and buggy out of a ditch. Most people cannot do this.

**Write About the Text** I used notes from my idea web to write a paragraph about Mighty Kate.

## Student Model: *Narrative Text*

Mighty Kate is stronger than other people. When she was baby, she lifted a doctor. Most babies can't do this. Mighty Kate lifted and threw a boulder. Most people can't lift and throw a boulder. She pulled a horse and buggy out of a ditch. Most people are not strong enough to do this. People know about Mighty Kate because she is stronger than most people.

## TALK ABOUT IT

COLLABORATE

### Text Evidence

**Draw a box** around a sentence that comes from the notes. Does Karim use this information as a clue?

### Grammar

**Circle** a sentence with the pronoun *this*. What does the pronoun refer to?

### Connect Ideas

**Underline** the sentences that tell about lifting and throwing a boulder. How can you combine the sentences using *but*?

### Your Turn

COLLABORATE

Write a paragraph to describe more actions that show Mighty Kate's strength.

>> *Go Digital!*
Write your response online. Use your editing checklist.

**?** **Essential Question**
What can you discover when you give things a second look?

>> *Go Digital*

16

**COLLABORATE**

**What do you see in the photograph? Look again. What is unusual about the map? Write in the chart what you can discover from giving a second look.**

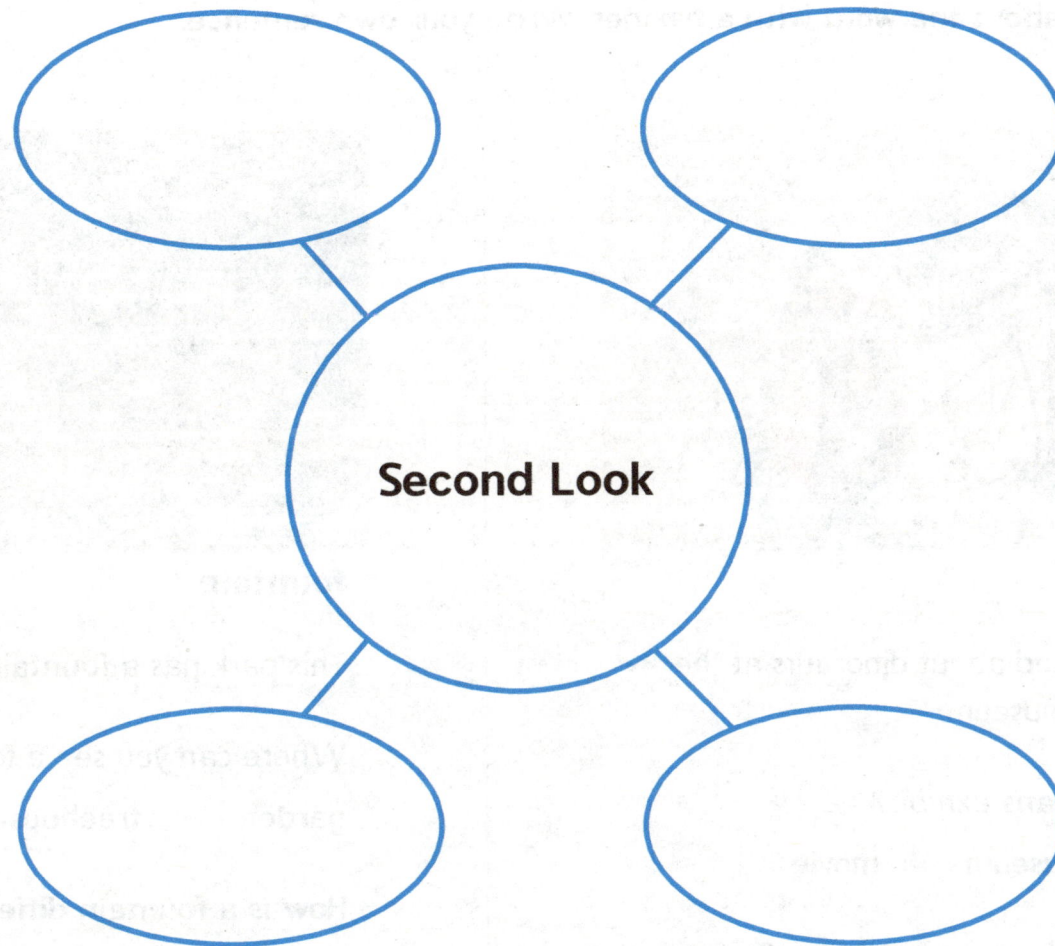

(empty oval)          (empty oval)

**Second Look**

(empty oval)          (empty oval)

**Discuss what you can discover from giving a second look at something. Use words from the chart. You can say:**

First I saw _____. From giving a second look, I discovered _____

_____.

Look at the picture. Read the word. Then read the sentence.
Talk about the word with a partner. Write your own sentence.

**exhibit**

My family learned about dinosaurs at the **exhibit** in the museum.

What word means *exhibit?*

display        museum        movie

**What exhibit do you want to see?**

I want to see an exhibit about _____

_____.

**fountain**

This park has a **fountain** in the garden.

Where can you see a fountain?

garden        treehouse        garage

**How is a fountain different from a statue?**

_____ comes out of a fountain.

# Words and Phrases: Multiple-Meaning Words

One meaning of *fair* is "an event where people show and get information."

What is a science fair?

A science **fair** is an event where people show and learn about science projects.

Another meaning of *fair* is "equal or right for everyone."

What is a fair way to play a game?

A **fair** way to play a game is to take turns.

**COLLABORATE** Talk with a partner. Look at the picture. Read the sentence. Circle the correct meaning of the word *fair*.

The family won lots of prizes at the school *fair*.

gathering          equal

The children cut the sandwich to divide it into *fair* parts.

gathering          equal

## COLLABORATE

### 1 Talk About It

Look at the picture. Read the title. Talk about what you see. Use these words.

**lizard    brown    missing**

Write about what you see.

This play is about _____

_____.

What color is the lizard?

The lizard is _____

_____.

What does the title tell you?

The title tells me the lizard is

_____

_____.

Take notes as you read the play.

# Where's Brownie?

## CAST

**SAM** *and* **ALEX JENSEN:** Twin sisters with different personalities. SAM is athletic and outgoing. ALEX is quiet and studious.

**NARRATOR:** One twin sister, ten years older.

**EVAN:** A classmate.

**NICK:** The building superintendent.

**NICKY:** Nick's young son.

### Essential Question

**?** **What can you discover when you give people or things a second look?**

Read about kids who use clues to find a missing lizard.

Elizabeth Buttler

## Scene One

*Setting: A bedroom in an apartment. SAM makes a poster at a messy desk. EVAN works at a clean desk. An empty terrarium and a wet, torn paper bag are nearby.*

**Narrator:** Whoever said "two heads are better than one" did not know my twin sister. She makes problems worse. Like when we lost Brownie, our pet chameleon ...

*(ALEX enters. SAM and EVAN cover up their work.)*

**Alex:** How was the science fair?

**Sam:** Mr. Rollins was surprised that my exhibit was so good. *(SAM tries to hide the empty terrarium from ALEX.)*

**Alex:** Where's Brownie? And why is Evan here?

*(EVAN and SAM text on hand-held devices.)*

**Alex:** How do I interpret your silence? I feel suspicious.

**Sam:** Brownie is missing. But Evan and I made posters!

**Sam:** We'll put the posters up at school tomorrow.

**Alex:** Do you think Brownie is at school?

**Sam:** Yes, I saw Brownie at school. He was in that bag.

**Alex:** The bottom of the bag is wet.

**Sam:** Maybe it got wet in the lobby. Nicky was playing in the fountain.

**Alex:** Hey! The bag has a rip at the bottom. Follow me. I think I know where Brownie is!

**Narrator:** We ran to the lobby.

## Text Evidence

**1 Sentence Structure** Ⓐ Ⓒ Ⓣ

Reread the Setting. What adjectives describe the paper bag? Circle the words. Write about it.

The paper bag is _____

and _____.

**2 Specific Vocabulary** Ⓐ Ⓒ Ⓣ

The word *like* means "for example." What example does the narrator give? Underline the text.

**3 Comprehension**
**Point of View**

Reread the description of the Narrator in the Cast section and the Narrator's dialogue. Which sister do you think is the narrator? Support your answer with text evidence.

I think the narrator is _____

because _____

_____

# Text Evidence

## 1 Specific Vocabulary ACT

Lizards are a type of reptile that has four legs and a long tail. How do you know that Brownie is a lizard? Circle the text that tells you.

I know Brownie is a lizard because

_____.

## 2 Sentence Structure ACT

Reread the first sentence in Evan's dialogue. Evan describes what he learns from his device. Underline the text that tells you what he learned.

Evan learned that _____

_____.

COLLABORATE

## 3 Talk About It

Discuss what Evan learned about chameleons. How do you know chameleons are a type of lizard? Support your answer with text evidence.

### Scene Two

*Setting: The lobby of the apartment building. A green plant is next to a fountain. NICKY is playing near the fountain. ALEX, SAM, and EVAN talk to NICK near a bulletin board.*

**Nick:** Why do you think Brownie is here?

**Sam:** Because he's not upstairs.

**Alex:** Brownie is a chameleon. We think he escaped from the bag.

**Nick.** Nicky! Did you see any brown lizards in the lobby?

**Nicky:** No.

**Evan:** *(looks at his device)* It says here that chameleons climb trees. They also prefer running water, like the fountain.

**Nick:** Nicky! Do you see any brown lizards in that tree?

**Nicky:** No.

**Nick:** Do you see any brown lizards in the fountain?

**Nicky:** No.

Elizabeth Buttler

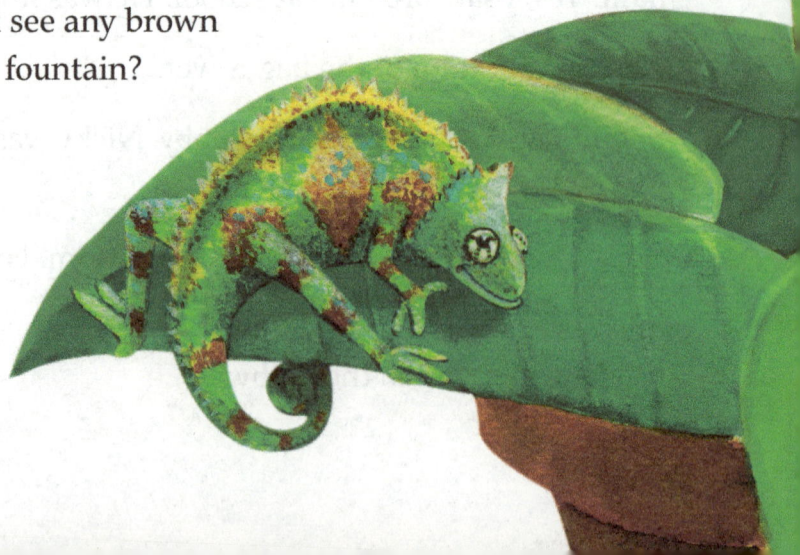

22

**Nick:** What else does that thing say?

**Sam:** Yeah, inquisitive minds want to know.

**Alex:** *(to SAM)* Don't you want to find Brownie? I hope you are not thinking "out of sight, out of mind".

**Sam:** He's a chameleon, Alex.

**Evan:** Listen to this! Chameleons change color to match their environments when they are confused or afraid.

**Alex:** Of course! Nicky, do you see any GREEN lizards?

**Nicky:** *(point to the tree)* There is one in the tree.

**Alex:** It's Brownie!

**Sam:** *(confused)* But Brownie is always brown.

**Alex:** That's because we put only brown things in his cage.

**Evan:** He needs a green plant.

**Sam:** And a little fountain.

**Narrator:** And, that is how we found our much-loved Brownie. All was well with the world once more!

## Make Connections

**?** How do Alex's and Evan's observations help them find Brownie? **ESSENTIAL QUESTION**

Think about a time when you gave a second look at someone or something. What did you discover? **TEXT TO SELF**

# Text Evidence

### 1 Sentence Structure **A C T**

Reread Nick's dialogue. What does the phrase *that thing* refer to? Underline the text that tells you in the previous page.

**COLLABORATE**

### 2 Talk About It

Discuss why Sam was confused. What did Evan and Sam suggest for Brownie? Write about it.

Sam was confused because _____

_____

_____.

### 3 Comprehension

### Point of View

Reread Narrator's dialogue. How does Narrator feel about Brownie? Circle the words that tell you.

Narrator feels _____

_____

# Respond to the Text

**Partner Discussion** Work with a partner. Read the questions about "Where's Brownie?" Show where you found text evidence. Write the page numbers. Then discuss what you read.

| | |
|---|---|
| **What does Alex learn about Brownie and what does she figure out?** | **Text Evidence** 🔍 |
| First, Alex sees the terrarium is _____. | Page(s): _____ |
| Then, Alex sees the paper bag is _____. | Page(s): _____ |
| Alex thinks Brownie is in _____. | Page(s): _____ |

| | |
|---|---|
| **How does the information Evan learns help the twins find Brownie?** | **Text Evidence** 🔍 |
| Evan learns chameleons _____. | Page(s): _____ |
| Then, Evan learns chameleons prefer _____. | Page(s): _____ |
| The children find Brownie by using _____ _____. | Page(s): _____ |

**Group Discussion** Present your answers to the group. Cite text evidence to justify your ideas. Listen to and discuss the group's opinions.

**Write** Work with a partner. Look at your notes about "Where's Brownie?" Write your answer to the Essential Question. Use text evidence to support your answer. Use vocabulary words from this week in your writing.

**How did Alex and Evan find Brownie?**

Alex figured out that Brownie is _____

_____.

Evan learned that chameleons _____

_____.

The children used the information to _____

_____.

**Share Writing** Present your writing to the class. Then talk about their opinions. Think about their ideas. Explain why you agree or disagree with their ideas. You can say:

I agree with _____.

I do not agree because _____.

Reggie

**Take Notes About the Text** I took notes about the text on the chart to respond to the prompt: *Add a dialogue between Sam and Alex in Scene One.*

pages 20–23

| Text Clues | Conclusion | New Dialogue |
|---|---|---|
| **Alex:** How was the science fair? <br> **Sam:** Mr. Rollins was surprised that my exhibit was so good. | Alex wants to know about the exhibit. <br> Sam tells Alex about how Mr. Rollins responded. | **Alex:** Alex asks Sam about the terrarium. <br> **Sam:** Sam tells Alex what was in the terrarium. <br> **Alex:** Alex asks Sam what Mr. Rollins said. <br> **Sam:** Sam tells Alex what Mr. Rollins liked about the exhibit. <br> **Alex:** Alex asks how Sam got the idea. <br> **Sam:** Sam tells Alex that he thought about what a chameleon wants. <br> **Alex:** Alex says Sam's idea is clever. |

**Write About the Text** I used my notes from my chart to write a new dialogue between Sam and Alex to add to Scene One.

## Student Model: *Narrative Text*

Alex: What did you have in the terrarium?

Sam: I put a waterfall, plants, rocks, and moss.

Alex: What did Mr. Rollins like about your exhibit?

Sam: He liked the waterfall, plants, rocks, and moss.

Alex: How did you get the idea?

Sam: I thought about what a chameleon wants in the terrarium.

Alex: That's very clever, Sam.

## TALK ABOUT IT

COLLABORATE

### Text Evidence

**Draw a box** around a line of dialogue that comes from the notes. What text clues did Reggie use to write the new dialogue?

### Grammar

**Circle** the pronoun *He*. Who does the pronoun *he* refer to?

### Condense Ideas

**Underline** the text that repeats in Sam's dialogue. How can you condense the sentences?

### Your Turn

COLLABORATE

Write a new dialogue for Scene Three. Have Sam and Alex talk about a plan to find Brownie if he is missing again. Use details that Sam and Alex learned in Scene Two.

>> *Go Digital!*
Write your response online. Use your editing checklist.

**? Essential Question**

What can people do to bring about a positive change?

>> *Go Digital*

MR. PRESIDENT HOW LONG MUST WOMEN WAIT FOR LIBERTY

**COLLABORATE**

What are the women in the photograph doing? What do the women want to change? Write words in the chart about what people do to make positive changes.

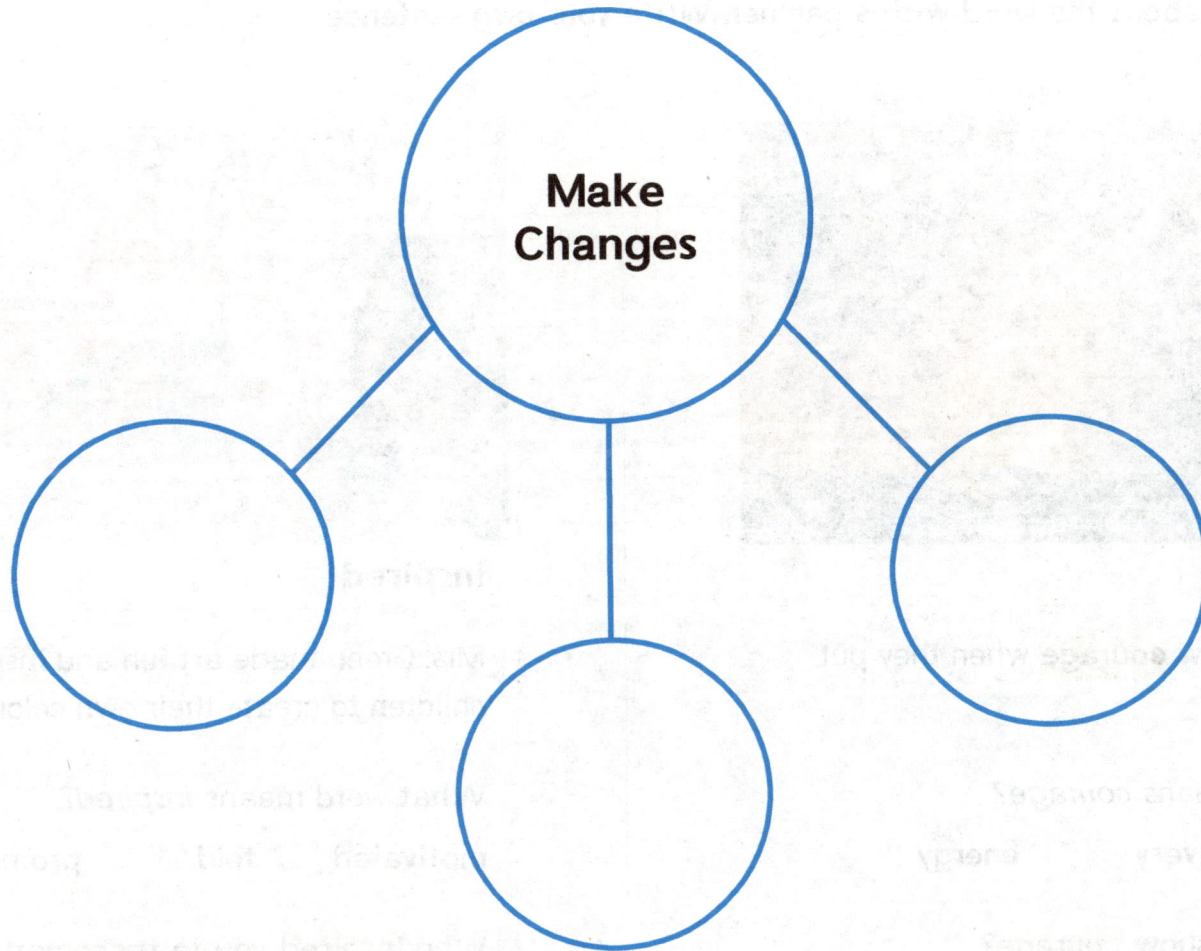

Make Changes

Discuss what people do to make positive changes. Use words from the chart. Complete these sentences.

The women want to change _____.

People _____ to make positive changes.

# More Vocabulary

COLLABORATE **Look at the picture. Read the word. Then read the sentence. Talk about the word with a partner. Write your own sentence.**

**courage**

Firefighters show <mark>courage</mark> when they put out fires.

What word means *courage?*

**fear**          **bravery**          **energy**

**When do you show <mark>courage</mark>?**

A person who has courage is not _____

_____.

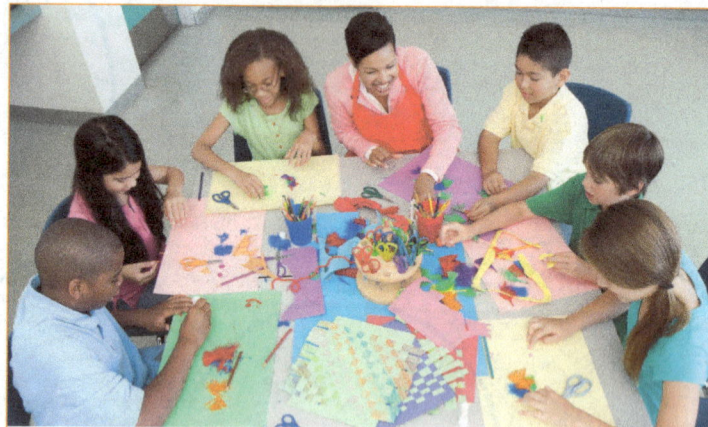

**inspired**

Mrs. Green made art fun and <mark>inspired</mark> the children to create their own colorful pictures.

What word means *inspired?*

**motivated**     **told**          **promised**

**Who <mark>inspired</mark> you to try something new?**

My _____ inspired me to

_____.

# Words and Phrases: *totally* and *speaker*

The word *totally* contains the suffix *–ly*. Totally means "completely."

Did Eva see the bee landing on her nose?

No, she was **totally** surprised.

The word *speaker* contains the suffix *–er*. Speaker means "a person who makes a speech."

What did the speaker tell the audience?

The **speaker** gave a speech about the importance of helping others.

**COLLABORATE** Talk with a partner. Look at the picture. Read the sentence. Write the word that completes each sentence.

The _____ is nervous before the speech. She will _____ to a large audience.

**speak**          **speaker**

The tire is _____ flat. The _____ repair cost will increase.

**totally**          **total**

## 1 Talk About It

Look at the images. Read the title. Discuss what you see. Use these words.

**Frederick Douglass**     **freedom** **change**    **leader**

Write about what you see.

This text is about _____

_____

What did Frederick Douglass do?

Frederick Douglass was a _____

_____.

Why is Frederick Douglass a leader?

Frederick Douglass is a leader because _____

_____.

Take notes as you read the text.

# FREDERICK DOUGLASS

## Freedom's Voice

### Essential Question

**?** **What can people do to bring about a positive change?**

Read about what Frederick Douglass did to make a positive change for African Americans.

Bettmann/Getty Images

## Growing Up with Slavery

Although Frederick Douglass was born into slavery, he became a great civil rights leader. At birth, he was named Frederick Bailey. He was enslaved, or lived in slavery, until he was twenty. Frederick's life was difficult. He was punished if he tried to defy his "master." The wife of a slave holder taught Frederick how to read. Perhaps his love of words, along with his **courage**, helped Frederick work for a better life.

▼ This picture shows a slave auction. This was a common event of Frederick's time.

## An Important Speech

In 1838, Frederick escaped to the North to find freedom. He married Anna Murray in New York City. Then they moved to New Bedford, Massachusetts.

Frederick changed his last name to Douglass to protect himself against slave catchers. He also discovered a group of abolitionists who shared his hope of ending slavery. He read about the abolition movement in William Lloyd Garrison's newspaper, *The Liberator*. The ideas of the movement **inspired** him. Frederick began speaking against slavery at church meetings.

Bettmann/Getty Images

## Text Evidence

**1 Sentence Structure** A C T

Reread the last sentence in the first paragraph. What two things helped Frederick work for a better life? Circle the text that tells you.

**2 Specific Vocabulary** A C T

The word *movement* means "a group of people who share and work for the same goal." What was the goal of the abolition movement? Underline the text.

The goal of the abolition movement

was _____

_____.

**3 Comprehension**
**Author's Point of View**

Reread the last paragraph. Put a box around the text that tells what inspired Frederick. What was he inspired to do?

Frederick was inspired to _____

_____

# Text Evidence 🔍

## 1 Sentence Structure Ⓐ Ⓒ Ⓣ

Reread the first sentence in the second paragraph. Underline the text that tells what made Frederick nervous.

Frederick was nervous because

_____.

## 2 Specific Vocabulary Ⓐ Ⓒ Ⓣ

The phrase *spoke from his heart* means "told his true feelings." Circle the text that tells what Frederick spoke about.

## 3 Comprehension
### Author's Point of View

Reread the last paragraph. Circle the words the author uses to describe Frederick's speeches. What is the author's point of view of Frederick?

The author's point of view is _____

_____

_____.

## New Opportunities

In 1841, The Massachusetts Anti-Slavery Society held a meeting in Nantucket. Frederick went to hear the speakers at the meeting. However, something totally unexpected happened. An abolitionist asked Frederick to speak at the meeting!

Frederick felt nervous standing in front of so many people. However, he spoke from his heart. He described the horrors of slavery. He was an inspiring speaker. At the end of his speech, everyone stood up and applauded!

After the meeting, William Lloyd Garrison hired Frederick to be a speaker for the Anti-Slavery Society.

Frederick traveled through New England and the Midwest giving passionate speeches. Frederick spoke with eloquence and dignity.

North Wind Picture Archives/Alamy Stock Photo

## More Success

In 1845, Frederick wrote an autobiography called *Narrative of the Life of Frederick Douglass, an American Slave*. The book was a huge success.

In the autobiography, Frederick revealed that he was a runaway slave, a fugitive. To protect himself against slave catchers, Frederick went to Great Britain on a speaking tour. He was very popular there.

In 1847, Frederick returned to the United States. He and his family moved to Rochester, New York. He started an unusual newspaper. *The North Star* was an abolitionist newspaper. It published articles about the anti-slavery cause and about the unequal status of women. Frederick also worked tirelessly to end segregation, or the separation of the races, in Rochester's schools.

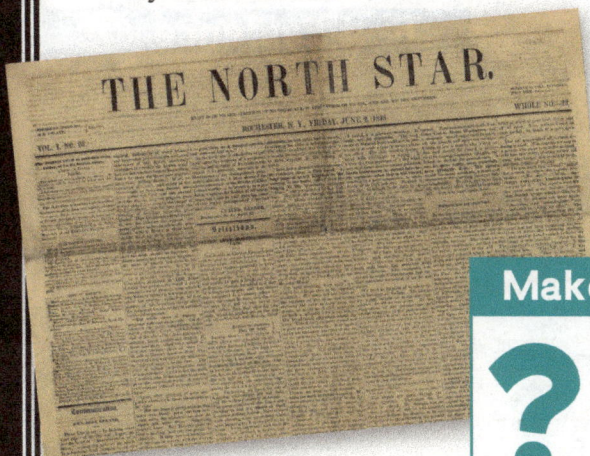

▲ Douglass's autobiography helped end slavery.

(t) Todd Bigelow/Aurora Photos; (b) Everett Collection Inc./Alamy Stock Photo

▲ Frederick Douglass and his wife published a newpaper called *The North Star*.

### Make Connections

? Talk about how Frederick Douglass helped African Americans. **ESSENTIAL QUESTION**

What did you do to help others or your community? What was the result? **TEXT TO SELF**

## Text Evidence

**1 Specific Vocabulary** Ⓐ Ⓒ Ⓣ

The word *revealed* means "showed or told something that was secret or hidden." What did Frederick reveal? Underline the text that tells you. Why did Frederick hide the information?

He hid the information because

_____

_____.

**2 Sentence Structure** Ⓐ Ⓒ Ⓣ

Reread the last sentence of the second paragraph. What does the pronoun *there* refer to? Circle the words.

**COLLABORATE**

**3 Talk About It**

Reread the third paragraph. Compare *The North Star* with another newspaper. Discuss why *The North Star* is an unusual newspaper.

# Respond to the Text

**Partner Discussion** Work with a partner. Read the questions about "Frederick Douglass: Freedom's Voice." Show where you found text evidence. Write the page numbers. Then discuss what you learned.

**COLLABORATE**

---

**What inspired Frederick Douglass to end slavery?**

Frederick read about the _____.

Frederick began to _____.

In 1841, Frederick spoke at _____.

**Text Evidence** 🔍

Page(s): _____

Page(s): _____

Page(s): _____

---

**What did Frederick Douglass do to speak out against slavery?**

Frederick worked as a speaker for the _____.

Then, he wrote _____.

In Rochester, New York, Frederick started _____

_____.

**Text Evidence** 🔍

Page(s): _____

Page(s): _____

Page(s): _____

---

**Group Discussion** Present your answers to the group. Cite text evidence for your ideas. Listen to and discuss the group's opinions.

**COLLABORATE**

**Write** Work with a partner. Look at your notes about "Frederick Douglass: Freedom's Voice." Write your answer to the Essential Question. Use text evidence to support your answer. Use vocabulary words from this week in your writing.

COLLABORATE

---

**What did Frederick Douglass do to make a positive change?**

Frederick worked to end _____.

He wrote a book about _____.

Frederick's newspaper wrote about _____.

Frederick changed the world by telling people _____

_____.

---

**Share Writing** Present your writing to the class. Discuss their opinions. Talk about their ideas. Explain why you agree or disagree with their ideas. You can say:

COLLABORATE

I agree with _____.

I do not agree because _____.

# Write to Sources

**Take Notes About the Text** I took notes about the text on the chart to answer the question: *Why does the author use sequence to write about Frederick Douglass?*

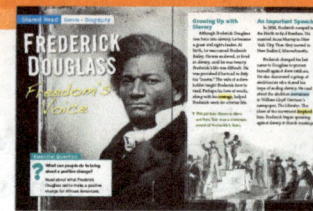

pages 32–35

Brandon

### First
Frederick Douglass lived in slavery. Life was difficult.

### Next
The wife of a slave holder taught him to read when he was young.

### Then
He escaped to the North in 1838. He spoke against slavery.

### Last
In 1841, he worked as a speaker with abolitionists. In 1847, he started a newspaper.

**Write About the Text** I used notes from my chart to write about why the author uses sequence to describe Frederick Douglass's life.

## Student Model: *Informative Text*

The author uses sequence to show how Frederick Douglass's life changed. As a child, Frederick Douglass lived in slavery. Life was difficult for him. When he was a young boy, the wife of a slave holder taught him to read. In 1838, he escaped to the North. He spoke out against slavery. Then, in 1841, he became a speaker. He worked with other abolitionists. Finally, in 1847, he started a newspaper. The author tells the events in order to shows that Frederick's life changed. His life changed from slavery to freedom.

## TALK ABOUT IT

COLLABORATE

### Text Evidence
**Draw a box** around a sentence that comes from the notes. Does this information support the main idea?

### Grammar
**Circle** the pronoun *him*. Who does the pronoun *him* refer to?

### Connect Ideas
**Underline** the two sentences that tell about what happened in 1838. How can you use the word *and* to connect the ideas?

### Your Turn
COLLABORATE

How did living in slavery lead Frederick Douglass to become a speaker? Use text evidence in your writing.

>> *Go Digital!*
Write your response online. Use your editing checklist.

### ? Essential Question

**Why are natural resources valuable?**

>> *Go Digital*

What are the workers doing with salt? How do people use salt? Why are natural resources important? Write words in the chart to tell about why natural resources are important.

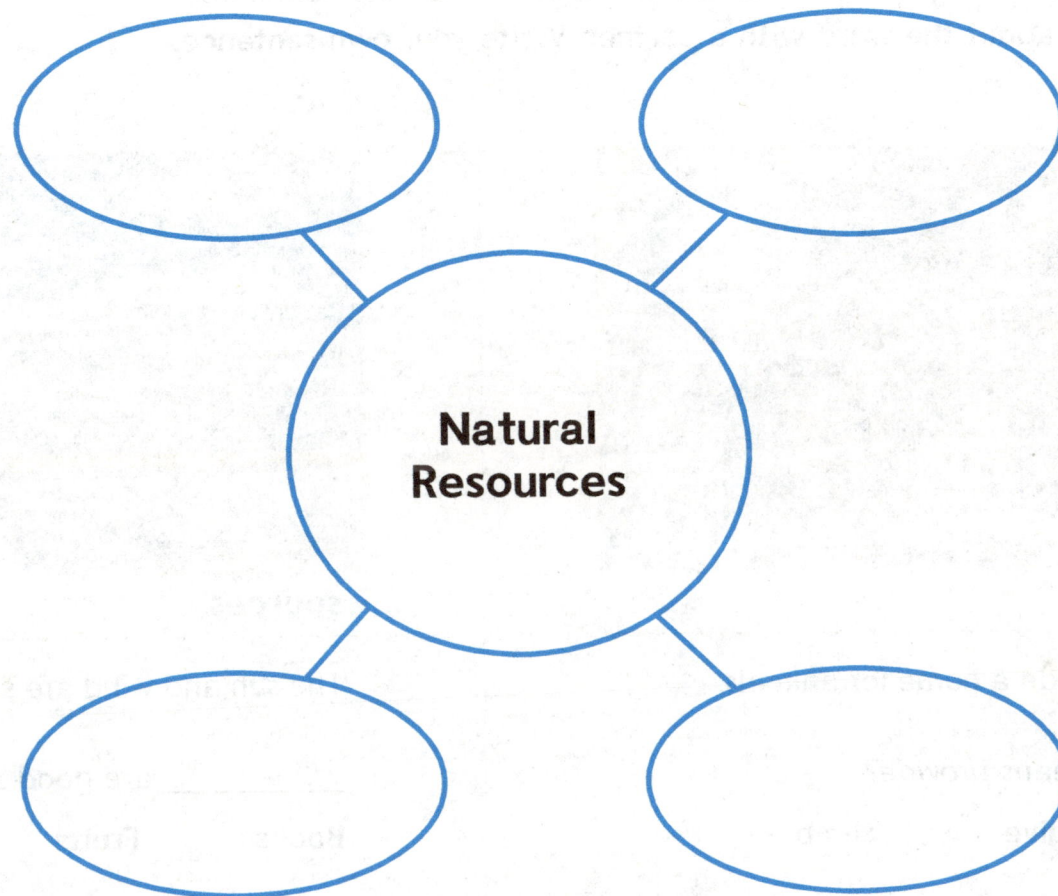

**Natural Resources**

Discuss reasons why natural resources are important. Use words from the chart. Complete the sentences.

Salt is an example of a _____.

People use natural resources to _____.

Natural resources are important because _____.

# More Vocabulary

**Look at the picture. Read the word. Then read the sentence. Talk about the word with a partner. Write your own sentence.**

**provide**

The trees **provide** a home for animals.

What word means *provide*?

**teach**　　　　**give**　　　**climb**

**What do your parents provide for you?**

My parents provide _____ for me.

**sources**

The sun and wind are **sources** of energy.

_____ are good *sources* of information.

**Books**　　　　**Fruits**　　　　**Shoes**

**What are good sources of light?**

_____ and _____

are sources of light.

# Words and Phrases: *run out* and *used up*

The phrase *run out* means "use all of something and have nothing left."

Is there any more peanut butter?

No, the peanut butter has **run out**.

The phrase *used up* also means "use all of something."

Is there battery power in the phone?

No, the battery power is **used up**.

**COLLABORATE** Talk with a partner. Look at the picture. Read the sentence. Write the word that completes each sentence.

We use gas to _____ cars. At this gas pump, the gas has _____.

**run out**          **run**

We _____ all the cereal in the box, so the cereal is now _____.

**used up**          **used**

**COLLABORATE**

## 1 Talk About It

Look at the photograph. Read the title. Discuss what you see. Use these words.

**power   nature   wind   resource**

**energy**

Write about what you see.

What do you see in the photograph?

The photograph shows _____

_____

_____

_____.

What kind of energy resource does the photograph show?

The photograph shows _____

_____

_____.

Take notes as you read the text.

44

# Power from NATURE

Wind turbines use wind to make energy.

## Essential Question

**?**

**Why are natural resources valuable?**

Read about the ways natural resources give us energy.

# Renewable and Nonrenewable Energy

Click! You just turned on a lamp. A power plant supplied the electricity for that lamp, and the electricity came from burning coal. Coal is a natural resource. It has to be extracted from the earth.

Natural resources are nature's gifts. They are metals and minerals, vegetation, soil, and animals. They include the things that are necessary for all life, such as water, air, and sunlight.

Natural resources provide energy. Energy makes things work. Energy runs our cars, computers, televisions, and machinery. Natural resources are energy **sources**.

There are two categories of energy sources. Renewable energy sources can be renewed, or continuously refilled. For example, sunlight and wind do not run out. In contrast, nonrenewable energy sources can be depleted, or used up. Fossil fuels, such as coal, natural gas, and oil, are nonrenewable energy sources. Nuclear energy is also nonrenewable because it requires uranium. There is a limited amount of uranium on earth.

**Cooling towers at an energy facility**

**A natural gas pipeline**

(bkgd) John A. Karachewski; (l) Digital Vision/Getty Images; (r) Keith Wood/The Image Bank/Getty Images

## Text Evidence

### 1 Sentence Structure A C T

Reread the second sentence. The sentence has two subjects. Circle the subjects. Underline the predicates. Rewrite the sentence as two sentences.

_____

_____

### 2 Comprehension
### Author's Point of View

Reread the first sentence in the second paragraph. What evidence does the author provide? Put a box around the text evidence.

### 3 Specific Vocabulary A C T

The word *categories* means "groups of people or things that are the same type." Circle the two categories of energy sources. How are the two categories different?

They are different because _____

_____.

45

## 1 Specific Vocabulary ⒶⒸⓉ

The word *usable* has the suffix *-able* and means "something you can use." Circle an example of usable energy in the paragraph.

An example of usable energy is

_____.

## 2 Sentence Structure ⒶⒸⓉ

Reread the first sentence in the third paragraph. Underline the predicate. What can create problems?

Problems can come from _____

_____.

## 3 Comprehension
### Author's Point of View

Reread the third paragraph. What is the author's point of view of using nonrenewable energy? Underline the sentence that tells you.

The author's point of view is _____

_____.

People have always used renewable energy. For example, sailors used wind to move ships. People burned wood to cook. In the 19th century, people began to use machines. Machines need a lot of energy to run. So, people had to develop energy from nonrenewable sources.

## Challenges and Problems

We use nonrenewable energy for many things. However, it is a challenge to get nonrenewable energy. Coal, gas, oil, and uranium have to be extracted from underground. We also need technology to transform natural resources into usable energy.

For example, gasoline has to be manufactured from oil and then delivered to customers.

Using nonrenewable energy poses problems. The energy sources can run out and pollute the environment. Burning coal produces gases that can poison the air. Some scientists argue that these gases heat up our atmosphere. They think global warming will cause glaciers to melt and sea levels to rise.

In addition, oil from spills often seeps into the ocean and pollutes the water. Nuclear energy creates dangerous waste.

### U.S. Energy Use from 1949–2010

*Types of Energy, Percentage of Energy Used by Year (approximate)*

| SOURCE OF ENERGY | 1949 | 1969 | 1989 | 2010 |
| --- | --- | --- | --- | --- |
| Fossil Fuels | 91% | 93% | 86% | 83% |
| Nuclear Power | 0% | 1% | 6% | 9% |
| Renewable Energy | 9% | 6% | 8% | 8% |

One solution to the challenge is renewable energy. It causes less pollution. However, it is currently difficult to produce a large amount of renewable energy.

## Solutions for the Future

Solar power, or power from the sun, shows promise. Solar panels absorb the sun's energy to **provide** heat. However, the sun's energy is less available at certain times and seasons. We need to figure out how to maximize our use of solar power and other renewable energy.

We can use nonrenewable energy more wisely. Government and private industry can help to protect natural resources and reduce pollution. We can turn off lights, TVs, and computers when we are not using them. Small efforts can create big changes in our energy future.

Solar panels on the roof make heat and electricity.

### Make Connections

**?** Talk about ways natural resources are valuable. **ESSENTIAL QUESTION**

How can you save energy? **TEXT TO SELF**

You can find rigs for drilling oil offshore.

(bkgd) morkeman/Vetta/Getty Images; (t) David J. Green/Alamy Stock Photo

# Text Evidence

**1 Specific Vocabulary** A C T

The word *promise* means "sign that something good will happen." What shows promise? Circle the text that tells you. What evidence tells you that solar power is a good energy source?

_____

_____

**2 Sentence Structure** A C T

Reread the third sentence in the third paragraph. What does the pronoun *them* refer to? Underline the text that tells you.

COLLABORATE

**3 Talk About It**

Discuss some ways people can use energy more wisely. Then write about them.

We can use energy more wisely by

_____

_____.

47

# Respond to the Text

**Partner Discussion** Work with a partner. Read the questions about "Power from Nature." Show where you found text evidence. Write the page numbers. Then discuss what you learned.

COLLABORATE

**What are natural resources?**

I read that natural resources provide _____.

**Text Evidence** 🔍

Page(s): _____

The two types of natural resources are _____.

Page(s): _____

We use natural resources to _____.

Page(s): _____

**What challenges do we have in using natural resources?**

To use nonrenewable energy we need to _____

_____.

**Text Evidence** 🔍

Page(s): _____

To use renewable energy we need to _____

_____.

Page(s): _____

We need to use energy wisely because _____.

Page(s): _____

**Group Discussion** Present your answers to the group. Cite text evidence for your ideas. Listen to and discuss the group's opinions.

COLLABORATE

**Write** Work with a partner. Look at your notes about "Power from Nature." Write your answer to the Essential Question. Use text evidence to support your answer. Use vocabulary words from this week's writing in your writing.

COLLABORATE

**Why are natural resources valuable?**

Natural resources are valuable because_____.

The two kinds of natural resources are _____.

One problem with nonrenewable energy is that _____

_____.

One problem with renewable energy is that _____

_____.

We need to use resources wisely because _____

_____.

**Share Writing** Present your writing to the class. Discuss their opinions. Talk about their ideas. Explain why you agree or disagree with their ideas. You can say:

COLLABORATE

I agree with _____.

I do not agree because _____.

# Write to Sources

Natalie

pages 44–47

**Take Notes About the Text** I took notes on the idea web to answer the question: *Is nonrenewable energy a good solution for our energy needs? Write about your opinion.*

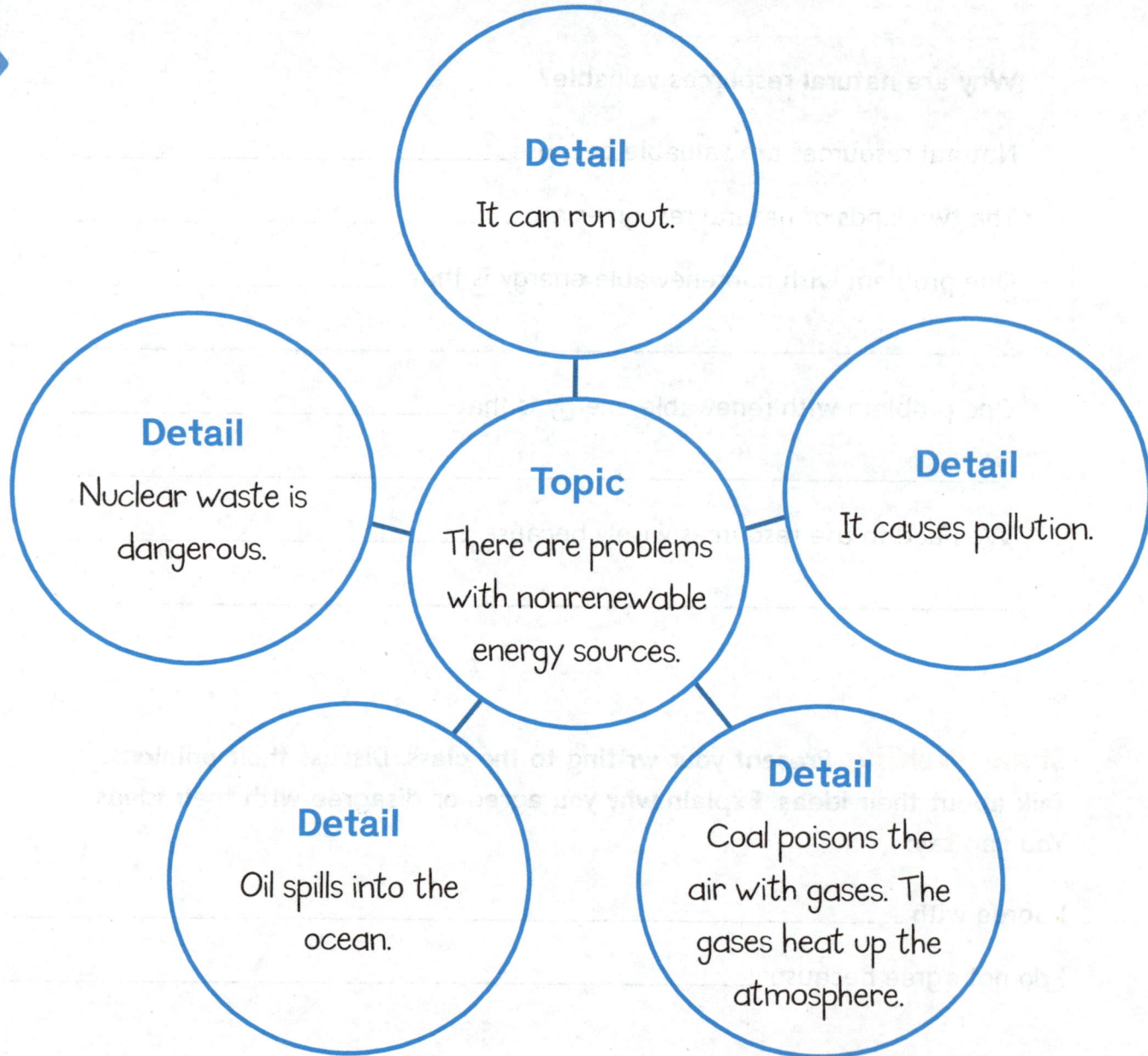

**Detail**
It can run out.

**Detail**
Nuclear waste is dangerous.

**Topic**
There are problems with nonrenewable energy sources.

**Detail**
It causes pollution.

**Detail**
Oil spills into the ocean.

**Detail**
Coal poisons the air with gases. The gases heat up the atmosphere.

**Write About the Text** I used notes from my idea web to write about my opinion on nonrenewable energy sources.

## Student Model: *Opinion*

In my opinion, nonrenewable energy is not good to use. It can run out. Nonrenewable energy causes pollution. When people burn coal, the coal can poison the air with gases. The gases heat up the atmosphere. Also, oil can spill. Sometimes oil spills into the ocean. Finally, nuclear waste is dangerous. For these reasons, people should use less nonrenewable energy.

## TALK ABOUT IT

COLLABORATE

### Text Evidence

**Draw a box** around a sentence that comes from the notes. Does this detail support Natalie's opinion?

### Grammar

**Circle** the verbs in the fourth sentence. What can poison the air?

### Condense Ideas

**Underline** the two sentences that tell about oil spills. How can you combine these sentences into one sentence to condense the ideas?

### Your Turn

COLLABORATE

In your opinion, did the author successfully explain why renewable energy sources are a good solution for our energy needs? Use text evidence in your writing.

>> *Go Digital!*
Write your response online. Use your editing checklist.

**What is the man in the photograph doing? How do you express yourself? Write words in the chart to tell how people express themselves.**

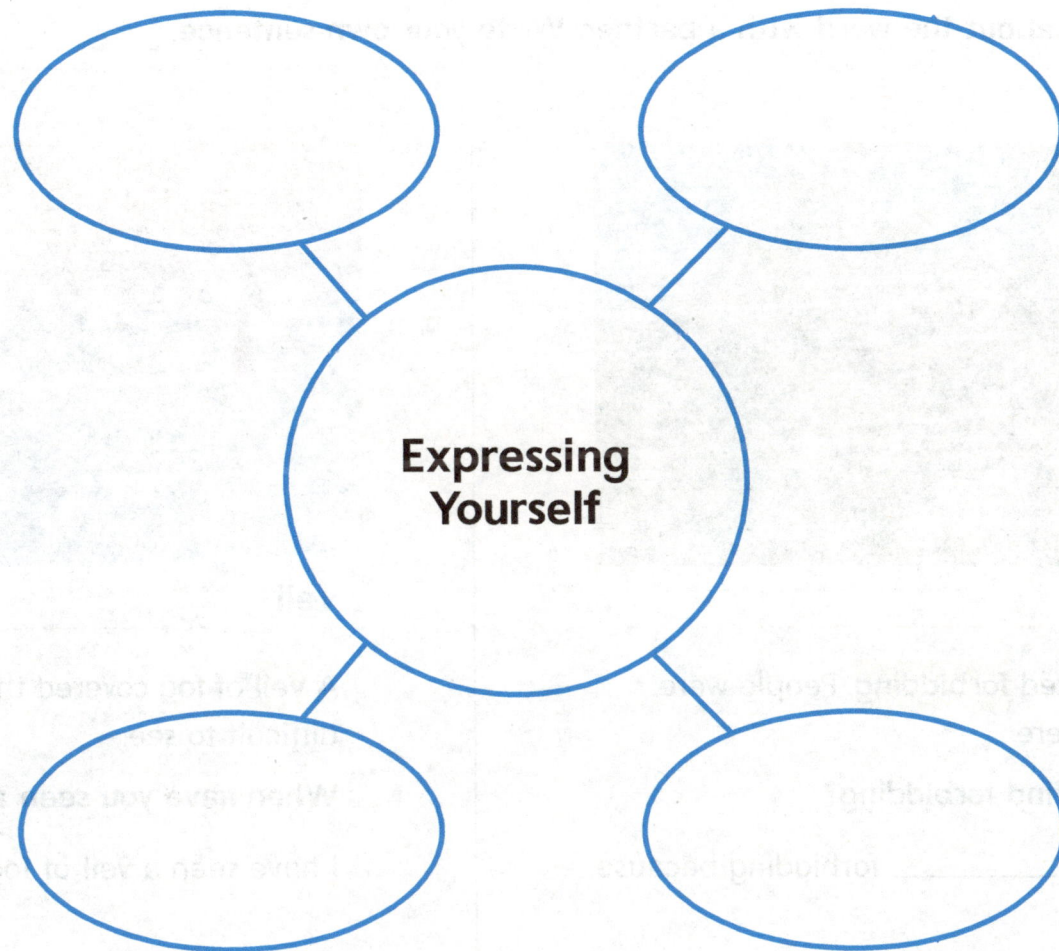

**Expressing Yourself**

**Discuss how people express themselves. Use words from the chart. For each way, you can say:**

I express myself by _____.

People express themselves by _____.

# More Vocabulary

Look at the picture. Read the word. Then read the sentence.
Talk about the word with a partner. Write your own sentence.

**forbidding**

The house looked **forbidding**. People were afraid to go there.

**What do you find forbidding?**

I find _____ forbidding because

I am afraid of _____.

**veil**

A **veil** of fog covered the bridge, so it was difficult to see.

**When have you seen a veil of fog?**

I have seen a veil of fog _____

_____.

Ules Barnwell/iStock/Getty Images; Brad Perks Lightscapes/Alamy

54

# Poetry Terms

## metaphor

A **metaphor** compares two things.

The lake is a mirror.

lake = mirror

## simile

A **simile** compares two different things. It uses *like* or *as.*

The horse is <u>as</u> white <u>as</u> snow.

The horse is white <u>like</u> snow.

## stanza

A **stanza** is a group of lines in a poem. The poem "We Have a Little Garden" by Beatrix Potter, has two stanzas. Each stanza has four lines.

### We Have a Little Garden

We have a little garden,
  A garden of our own,
And every day we water there
  The seeds that we have sown.

We love our little garden,
  And tend it with such care,
You will not find a faded leaf
  Or blighted blossom there.

Ingram Publishing/SuperStock; Ken Karp/McGraw-Hill Education; Comstock/PictureQuest; JFCreative/Getty Images

COLLABORATE

### 1 Talk About It

Read the title. Discuss the season in the photograph. Is the season in the title different from the photograph? Explain your answer.

The season is different because _____

_____.

### 2 Specific Vocabulary ⒶⒸⓉ

The word *setting* means "the sun is disappearing at the end of the day." What has changed about the setting of the sun? Underline the text.

The sun is setting _____

than before.

### 3 Literary Element
### Simile

Reread line 5. What does the poet compare the lake to? Circle the text.

The poet compares the lake to _____

_____.

# How Do I Hold the Summer?

The sun is setting sooner now,
     My swimsuit's packed away.
How do I hold the summer fast,
     Or ask it, please, to stay?

The lake like cold, **forbidding** glass—
     The last sailboat has crossed.
Green leaves, gone gold, fall, float away—
     Here's winter's **veil** of frost.

### Essential Question

**?**  **How do you express something that is important to you?**

Read how a poet describes something important.

I thought of ice and barren limbs—
　　Last winter's snow so deep!
I know I cannot ball up light,
　　And green grass just won't keep,

So I'll search for signs of summer,
　　Hold memories of each—
Soft plumes of brown pressed in a book,
　　The pit of one ripe peach,

Each instance of a cricket's chirp,
　　And every bird's sweet call,
And store them up in a poem to read
　　When snow begins to fall.
— Maya Jones

## Make Connections

**?** Talk about what the speaker
wants to tell the reader.
How does the speaker say it?
ESSENTIAL QUESTION

Compare the speaker's way of
saying things to the way you
say things. TEXT TO SELF

# Text Evidence

**1 Specific Vocabulary** (A)(C)(T)

The word *pit* means "the seed of
a fruit." Circle the word that tells
the type of fruit. What is the pit a
reminder of?

The pit is a reminder of _____.

**2 Comprehension**
**Theme**

Reread the second stanza on the
page. What does the speaker want
to do? Underline the text.

The speaker wants to _____

_____.

COLLABORATE

**3 Talk About It**

Reread the last stanza. Discuss
what the speaker will do during
winter. Underline the text.

During winter the speaker will _____

_____.

(tr) Tim Grollimund; (bkgd) Stephen Frink/Corbis

# Respond to the Text

**Partner Discussion** Work with a partner. Read the questions about "How Do I Hold the Summer?" Show where you found text evidence. Write the page numbers. Then discuss what you read.

**COLLABORATE**

---

**What does the speaker see?**

The speaker sees that the sun is _____.

Green leaves change to a _____.

Soon winter's _____.

**Text Evidence** 🔍

Page(s): _____

Page(s): _____

Page(s): _____

---

**How will the speaker hold onto summer?**

The speaker thinks about _____.

The speaker decides to search for _____
_____.

To hold onto memories, the speaker _____
_____.

**Text Evidence** 🔍

Page(s): _____

Page(s): _____

Page(s): _____

---

**Group Discussion** Present your answers to the group. Cite text evidence for your ideas. Listen to and discuss the group's opinions.

**COLLABORATE**

**Write** Work with a partner. Look at your notes about "How Do I Hold the Summer?" Write your answer to the Essential Question. Use text evidence to support your answer. Use vocabulary words from this week in your writing.

**How does the speaker express something that is important?**

The speaker is sad that the summer is _____

because _____.

The speaker wants to _____

_____.

The poem helps the speaker express her feelings about _____

_____.

**Share Writing** Present your writing to the class. Discuss their opinions. Talk about their ideas. You can say:

I agree with _____.

I do not agree because _____.

# Write to Sources

**Take Notes About the Text** I took notes about the text on the chart to answer the question: *What similes does the poet use in the poem? What do the similes mean?*

Esther

**Text Clue**

"The lake like cold, forbidding glass"

**Text Clue**

Uses "like" or "as" so it is a simile.

**Conclusion**

The poet compares the lake to cold, forbidding glass. In fall, the lake is cold for swimming.

**Write About the Text** I used notes from my chart to write a paragraph about a simile in the poem.

The poet describes the lake in the fall. She writes, "the lake is like cold, forbidding glass." The poet uses the word "like", so it is a simile. The poet compares the lake to glass. I know that glass is hard. The poet uses the word "cold". So, cold glass means cold water in the fall. The poet also uses the word "forbidding". I know that something forbidding is not welcoming. It is not fun to swim in cold, hard water. This simile tells about the lake. It tells what the lake is like in fall.

## TALK ABOUT IT

**COLLABORATE**

### Text Evidence

**Draw a box** around a sentence that comes from a text clue in the notes. Does this information support that the poet uses a simile?

### Grammar

**Circle** the pronoun *it* in the third sentence. What does this pronoun refer to?

### Condense Ideas

**Underline** the last two sentences. How can you combine these sentences into one sentence to condense the ideas?

### Your Turn

**COLLABORATE**

Identify and explain a metaphor in the poem. Use text evidence in your writing.

**>> Go Digital!**
Write your response online. Use your editing checklist.